# Wearing the Mask
## Dramas for Youth

Tim Shoemaker

*To my wife, Cheryl ... for believing in me.*

Scripture quotations are taken from the HOLY BIBLE, NEW INTERNATIONAL VERSION®. NIV®. Copyright © 1973, 1978, 1984 by International Bible Society. Used by permission of Zondervan Publishing House. All rights reserved.

Copyright © 1999 Concordia Publishing House
3558 S. Jefferson Avenue, St. Louis, MO 63118-3968
Manufactured in the United States of America

Educational institutions, teachers, or churches who purchase this product may reproduce pages for classroom use, for use in parish-education programs, or for use in worship settings. Material is intended for use by purchaser in the purchaser's local church only. As the purchaser, you may make as many copies of the scripts as are needed for performance in your local church only. You may perform the sketches as often as you wish at no additional cost. Scripts and performance rights are not transferable between churches and cannot be resold. You may not use the sketches for any commercial or fundraising purpose, and usage rights do not extend to video, radio, television, or film.

All rights reserved. Except as noted above, no part of this publication may be reproduced, stored in a retrieval system, or transmitted, in any form or by any means, electronic, mechanical, photocopying, recording or otherwise, without the prior written permission of Concordia Publishing House.

1  2  3  4  5  6  7  8  9  10      08  07  06  05  04  03  02  01  00  99

# Table of Contents

| | |
|---|---:|
| Introduction | 5 |
| Wearing the Mask | 7 |
| The Dating Game | 14 |
| Thrill Ride | 22 |
| The Edge | 30 |
| The Palm Reader's Prediction | 39 |
| The Fabulous Female | 46 |
| The Magnificent Male | 53 |
| Perfect Combination | 58 |
| Emergency Room | 63 |
| The Truth about Hell | 70 |
| The Truth about Heaven | 77 |
| Getting There | 85 |
| Lisa's Letter | 92 |

# Introduction

Student culture, with all its diversity, has increasingly become a challenge to the Church. How do you creatively and relevantly reach a group so different from the rest of the church's population?

To bemoan the fact that students are a part of the post-Christian era only secludes ministries. Instead, we remember that God has the Church in a strategic position to deeply impact the students. The strategy calls for innovation, excellence, and a God-given desire to clearly communicate the life-changing message of the Gospel. In essence, we need to push the limits.

In His ministry, Jesus often "pushed the limits." He knew how to get a crowd to listen. He'd start with a story: "There was a certain man ..." The crowd could visualize the story as Jesus told it, just as if it were being played out in front of them. They identified with it.

Today's culture is similar. "Generation X" and generations that follow are narrative generations; they live by and learn by stories. Dramas are visual stories that catch the interest of the crowd and prepare their hearts for the message. A well-performed sketch can open a door to the Gospel in a way few other things can.

*Wearing the Mask* is designed for a mixed group of high school students: the Christian and the non-Christian. It is intended for outreach. Make sure the players have rehearsed their parts and know them well; this is ministry.

The sketches are not so "predictably Christian" that your audience will be bored. Neither do they preach. The preaching is your job as youth minister or pastor. Sometimes the sketch will end without giving the "right" point of view. This will give you a springboard to unfold the truth of God's love and mercy, as suggested in the pastor's notes and questions for discussion.

The sketches in *Wearing the Mask* push the limits in some cases. But then, they have to. There's a lot at stake. We're fighting for the souls of our youth. These sketches won't turn your audience off; they may just get them thinking. And when it's time for you to get up to speak to the group, they'll be listening. So get up and "speak the Word with great boldness" (Acts 4:29b).

In other words, push the limits.

Tim Shoemaker, Author
Pastor John Zivojinovic, Youth Pastor

# Wearing the Mask

**Purpose:** A farcical look at the length people go to in order to "blend in"

**Theme:** Individuality

**Scripture:** Genesis 3:6–10, 21; Romans 12:2

**Time:** 5–7 minutes

**Cast:** **Carol Webster *(Mom)*** —mother of two teenagers

**Gary**—her teenage son, trying to fit in with friends

**Kathy**—her teenage daughter, trying to fit in with friends

**Beth**—Kathy's friend

**Robin**—Kathy's friend

**Costumes:** Kathy and Gary wear modern clothes that look sharp, but can easily be adjusted to look sloppy. Beth and Robin wear clothes similar to Kathy's "sloppy" look. Carol wears modern "mom"-type clothes

**Props:** Masks for the four teens (ski masks work well), comfortable chairs, an end table, a lamp, a newspaper, a grocery bag

**Lighting:** General

**Sound:** Doorbell

**Setting:** The Websters' family room. The furniture should be arranged as a living room, chairs facing the audience

# Wearing the Mask

*MOM is in a chair, reading a newspaper, as KATHY ENTERS.*

#### KATHY

*(Casually)* Mom, I'm going out.

#### MOM

*(Looking up from paper)* Where are you going?

#### KATHY

Just out with some friends.

#### MOM

Don't be late. *(She pauses, looks at KATHY, then adds)* You look nice.

#### KATHY

*(Suddenly worried)* You think so? *(She pretends to look in a wall mirror. Frantically, she messes her hair a little, untucks her shirt, and opens an extra button at the top)*

#### MOM

*(Watching in surprise)* Honey, what are you doing? I said you looked nice.

#### KATHY

That's what got me worried.

#### MOM

You don't *want* to look nice?

#### KATHY

*(As if she can't believe she has to explain)* Mom, *nice* girls aren't in real high demand these days. *(She pulls her mask from her pocket.)*

#### MOM

Oh, no. You're not wearing that again! *(KATHY ignores her and pulls the mask over her face.)* Kathy, that isn't you. Take off the mask.

#### KATHY

*(Lifts mask off face to about hairline)* What, and go out looking like this? I don't think so.

#### MOM

*(Trying to be convincing)* If those people are really your friends, they should like you for who you really are, not for who you pretend to be. Kathy, let them see the real you. Don't wear a mask.

#### KATHY

I'd rather be dead. *(DOORBELL rings.)* Oh, they're here. *(She pulls mask over her face and rushes to open the door.)*

ROBIN and BETH ENTER and take a step or two into the room. Both are dressed similarly to Kathy, and wearing masks. MOM still looks concerned.

#### MOM

*(Gets up from chair and crosses to girls. She puts her hand on ROBIN's shoulder.)* Come in, Beth. *(Looking over at BETH)* You too, Robin.

#### ROBIN

Ah, I'm Robin.

#### BETH

And I'm Beth.

#### MOM

*(Looks from one to the other for a moment)* Oh, I'm sorry girls, I can't seem to tell you girls apart. In fact, I was just talking to Kathy about—

#### KATHY

*(Interrupting)* Mom, we gotta go. We'll talk later. *(Turns quickly for door)* C'mon guys, we're late.

*KATHY, BETH, and ROBIN EXIT. MOM stands there for a moment, then goes back to her chair and sits down, looking sad. GARY ENTERS.*

### GARY

*(In a rush and carrying a grocery bag)* Hi, Mom. I'm going out with some friends.

### MOM

*(With mild protest)* But you just got home ... and you haven't eaten yet.

### GARY

*(Holds up bag and grins)* I grabbed a snack; I'll eat on the way. *(Looks out the window)* Hey, they're here already. I won't have time to change!

### MOM

Change? What's wrong with what you're wearing? You look very nice.

### GARY

*(As he untucks his shirt and messes his hair)* I'm not going to church, I'm going out with friends. Can I borrow an earring?

### MOM

*(Firmly)* No, you cannot! Why did you pull out your shirt and mess your hair? You're going out.

### GARY

Exactly.

### MOM

What?

### GARY

You just answered your own question—I'm going out, that's why I, ah, rearranged things a little. *(He pulls ski mask out of his pocket.)*

#### Mom

*(Seeing the mask)* Oh, no. Not the mask!

#### Gary

*(As he pulls it on over his face)* Yep—just like American Express—"Don't leave home without it."

#### Mom

It looks like you're going to rob a gas station. What's wrong with being who you are?

#### Gary

*(Lifting up mask so his face can be seen)* Mom, without my mask, I'm nobody.

#### Mom

*(Frustrated)* So you dress like everybody, you look like everybody, you act like everybody, and then you're somebody?

#### Gary

Exactly. Gotta run now. Bye, Mom. *(Gives her a quick hug.)*

#### Mom

*(Still has her arms around him. As they start to separate, she keeps a hand on each of his shoulders to hold him so she can talk to him face to face.)* Be yourself, Gary. If your friends don't like who you really are, find new friends.

#### Gary

*(Pretending to be serious)* Hey, great idea, Mom. I'll try that. I'll let them see who I really am and hey, if they don't like me, well, I'll just dump those friends and stop by Wal-Mart on the way home and pick up some new ones.

#### Mom

Gary, I just—

#### GARY

*(Interrupting)* No, it's a great idea. Maybe I'll try that greeter they have there. I'll bet he'd like to be my friend.

#### MOM

Gary, I just mean that real friends are the ones you can be yourself with.

#### GARY

*(Shakes head and laughs as he pulls away from her)* Mom, you're funny. I gotta go. Bye.

*GARY waves, pulls mask over his face, and EXITS. MOM shakes her head and EXITS opposite.*

# Wearing the Mask

## A Note to the Pastor or Youth Leader:

Masks come in a variety of styles, a variety of sizes. Whether consciously or subconsciously, we wear them to hide from others, from ourselves, from God. We wear them to blend in. We wear them to present ourselves as someone we're not. Problems arise not so much from the person we then present, but rather from the person we hide.

In the sketch, Carol was most concerned that her son and daughter were not being themselves; they were putting on masks to blend in with their friends. Wanting to blend in is not, in and of itself, a sin. But doing so can keep us from celebrating and using the unique personalities and gifts that God has given us, and, at times, keep us from staying true to our faith and beliefs.

But we also need to be concerned about putting on a mask before God; attempting to hide or disguise our sinful nature, desires, or actions. Far too often we are like Adam and Eve after eating the fruit in the garden. They tried to mask their shamefulness with fig leaves, and tried to hide when God called out to them. God knows our sins and, as a just God, must punish them. But out of His graciousness, through the death and resurrection of His Son, He provides new clothes—masks—of grace and righteousness which we receive through Baptism. We can then, as individual and unique members of His creation, live in the forgiveness of Christ.

## Questions for Study and Discussion:

1. Why did Kathy and Gary want to wear masks?

2. What masks do you put on? Why?

3. Are masks ever beneficial? When are they dangerous?

4. In what ways does Christ give you a new identity and purpose for living?

# The Dating Game

**Purpose:** To explore misconceptions about dating and relationships

**Theme:** Dating; honesty

**Scripture:** 1 John 3:18–20

**Time:** 5–7 minutes

**Cast:** **Dave**—a high school senior; confident and smooth talking

**Sean**—a freshman; unsure of himself when it comes to dating

**Lisa**—an attractive high school student; a nice girl who just went through a breakup with her boyfriend

**Julie**—a flirt

**Students**—optional two or three students to sit at far end of table from Dave and Sean to give a lunchroom look; girls would be best

**Costumes:** Contemporary casual clothing, appropriate to character; Lisa could look more dressed up.

**Props:** Several tables and chairs, trays or lunch bags

**Lighting:** General

**Sound:** No sound effects necessary

**Setting:** A school cafeteria. Tables are set up in a long row. Extra students sit at the far end. They should be careful not to distract from the focus of the sketch.

# The Dating Game

*Several students are sitting at the far end of a long table. SEAN is sitting by himself at the downstage end of the table. DAVE ENTERS, holding a tray. He approaches SEAN at the table.*

#### DAVE

All right, Sean ... time for you to tell ol' Dave how you're doing. *(He sits down at the table.)*

#### SEAN

I'm okay. Classes are pretty good this semester. I think I may even make the honor roll.

#### DAVE

I don't care about *that*. I mean how are you doing with the opposite sex? *(He smiles and nods toward the girls at the other end of the table.)*

#### SEAN

Well ... uh ... I'm doing good.

#### DAVE

Sean, my boy ... when you were a brand-new baby freshman, who was that upperclassman who helped show you the ropes, the guy who was there for you just like he was your big brother?

#### SEAN

Well, that was you, Dave.

#### DAVE

Yeah, so this is "big brother" Dave you're talking to. You can trust me. What's this "doing good" with the girls stuff? When's the last time you were out on a date?

#### SEAN

I'm out with girls all the time. A whole bunch of us usually get together and—

#### DAVE

*(Interrupting)* Hey, I'm not talking about "a whole bunch of you getting together." I'm talking about just *you*, with just *one* girl, going out someplace by *yourselves*.

#### SEAN

Uh ... like a "date" date?

#### DAVE

*(Nodding)* A "date" date.

#### SEAN

Well ... Umm ... *(Looks down like he is concentrating.)*

#### DAVE

There hasn't been one, has there?

#### SEAN

Well, not exactly.

#### DAVE

Not exactly?

#### SEAN

*(Defensively)* Well, I'm working on it. I just haven't asked anyone yet.

#### DAVE

Listen, Sean. Before you know it, I'll be graduating. I won't be around to help you. So you've got to learn now how this dating game is played.

#### SEAN

"Dating game"?

#### DAVE

That's right. Dating is a game. Like Monopoly. You gotta roll the dice, take some chances. You start to move around ... here ... there ... all over. You land somewhere you like, you invest a little money and buy the property. Just like Monopoly. See what I mean?

#### SEAN

Not really.

#### DAVE

Listen. You move around ... get to know this girl and that girl. Invest a little time and attention in them. Sooner or later they pay off. *(LISA ENTERS. She is carrying a tray with food on it. She hesitates like she is looking for a place to sit.)* Hey look ... speaking of Monopoly, here comes "Park Place." No, make that "Boardwalk." Oh, would I love to put up a motel on her property! *(LISA starts to slowly walk toward the table.)* Okay, Sean. Stay quiet and take notes. *(LISA is walking by the table. DAVE stands to meet her. He looks sincere and concerned.)* Hey, Lisa. How ya doing?

#### LISA

*(Looks down to the floor.)* I'm doing all right.

#### DAVE

*(Looks both ways discreetly.)* Hey, I heard about you and Kevin breaking up. I just wanted you to know how bad I felt. I think you got a pretty raw deal.

#### LISA

*(Puts tray down on table and looks up at him.)* Thanks, Dave. I thought all the guys would be taking his side on it.

#### DAVE

*(Shaking his head)* My sister had a boyfriend like him once. *(He puts his hand on her shoulder.)* He left her high and dry too—but not before she was pregnant.

#### LISA

Oh, no!

#### DAVE

*(Looks down, emotional)* Yeah, it was pretty tough. Nearly broke my mom's heart. I've seen what a guy like Kevin can do to a girl, and to her family. Anyway, I think it helps me understand just a little of what you must be going through.

#### LISA

*(Putting her hand gently on DAVE's arm)* Thank you, Dave. That really means a lot to me. So how did your sister handle it? I mean, what did she do?

#### DAVE

*(Closes eyes tight, as if trying to block out a horrible memory)* Well, she ... ah ... she didn't cope very well. *(Pause, struggling not to cry)* She ... ah ... she took a bottle of pills.

#### LISA

Oh, no! *(DAVE still has his eyes closed tight. He just nods. LISA puts her arms around him and hugs him tight. She doesn't let him go. DAVE wraps his arms around her and returns the hug. They stand there holding each other. DAVE is facing the audience and SEAN. LISA has her back to the audience.)* That must have been awful!

#### DAVE

If you only knew. *(He looks over LISA's shoulder and flashes SEAN a big smile and a "thumbs up" sign. LISA and DAVE let go of each other, but LISA still keeps one hand on his arm. They turn so their sides are to the audience as they face each other. DAVE sniffs, wipes eyes.)* Hey, I feel terrible. Here I wanted to cheer you up, and you end up trying to make me feel better.

### Lisa

Me? I didn't do anything.

### Dave

That's not true. You did more than you know. Kevin was a fool to let you go. *(Pauses, looks down for a brief, shy moment, then looks back at LISA.)* Hey, I have an idea. Why don't I take you somewhere Saturday night? I want to give you a chance to get some of this off your chest. You need to do that for yourself. Just don't let me get started about my sister—I'll cry all over my dinner.

### Lisa

*(Thoughtfully)* You know, I think that's just what I need. I'd love to go, Dave. You're a pretty special guy, you know that? You're always thinking of others instead of yourself.

### Dave

*(Looks down shyly, then looks up)* I'll pick you up at 6:00.

### Lisa

*(Smiles)* Okay, I'll see you then! *(She picks up her tray and happily goes to sit with the girls at the far end of the table.)*

### Dave

*(Sits down, proud)* Now *that*, my boy, is how you play the game!

### Sean

Hey, I'm sorry about your sister. I never knew.

### Dave

Sister? I don't even have a sister. That was all part of playing the game. You tell them what they want to hear if it gets you where you want to go ... and I'm going to "Boardwalk!"

### Sean

You—you mean none of that was true?

**DAVE**

Well, I never had a sister, but the part about me wanting to take her out on Saturday night sure is true. The important thing is that you see how the game works. Treat the girls nice, even the ones who aren't so cute. Who knows? They may have a good-looking friend. Are you catching this? *(SEAN nods.)* Good. Remember: listen; act sincere, sympathetic, and caring. Trust me, it pays off big in a short time!

*JULIE ENTERS. As she walks by DAVE she gives him a flirty smile.*

**JULIE**

Hi, Dave!

**DAVE**

*(He smiles back)* Hi, Julie. You are looking absolutely ravishing this afternoon.

*JULIE flashes him another flirty smile and EXITS.*

**DAVE**

*(Leaning over and talking to SEAN again)* And never burn any bridges. You never know which ones will pay off. *(Stands up)* You got it?

**SEAN**

*(Nodding)* I think so.

**DAVE**

Good. I'm going to check up on you. You get a "date" date for this weekend, all right?

**SEAN**

*(With new determination and confidence)* All right!

**DAVE**

That's it! If you wanna win, you gotta play the game!

*EVERYONE EXITS.*

# The Dating Game

## A Note to the Pastor or Youth Leader:

Relationships are an essential part of our lives. Whether with peers, people older, or people younger, these interactions with others shape much of our perceptions of our world and ourselves. Honest relationships, then, are incredibly important.

Honest relationships with the opposite sex, however, can be incredibly difficult—especially early in one's dating "career." Because of differences in our thought processes, views on the world, and intuitions and perceptions, situations and conversations often get damaged in translation. This happens more often when one party has ulterior motives, or a skewed view on the place or importance of the conversation.

Although social scientists, psychologists, and other experts have been studying gender differences and relationships for years, miscommunication happens without fail. Why? Because as sinful, fallible creatures, there is only so much we can accomplish on our own. But the problem is solved because Christ has earned forgiveness for us through His death and resurrection. In Baptism, He gives us a new and clean heart, one filled with His love and Spirit. When we speak and act out of a response to this love and Spirit, we live in accord with each other. With God's continued help, we may strengthen and develop our relationships with others, especially those of the opposite sex, to His glory.

## Questions for Study and Discussion:

1. Explain how Dave views relationships. Do you agree with this mindset? Why?

2. Based on the conversation Dave has with Lisa, how do you think their date—and potential relationship—will turn out?

3. How do you approach relationships? Do you think you present an honest picture of yourself to others?

4. How will honest living and loving affect your relationships with friends of the same sex? Opposite sex? Family?

5. Is your relationship with God honest? Describe how God—through Christ—has honestly and fully shown His love for you.

# Thrill Ride

**Purpose:** To explore misconceptions about dating and relationships

**Theme:** Dating; treatment of others

**Scripture:** 1 Peter 1:13–16

**Time:** 5–7 minutes

**Cast:** **Brian**—high school student, frustrated by dating

**Kyle**—high school student, uses girls he dates

**Chad**—a friend of Kyle

**Debbie**—good-looking high school student, a flirt

**Costumes:** Contemporary clothing, appropriate to character

**Props:** A bench, or several chairs

**Lighting:** General

**Sound:** No sound effects necessary

**Setting:** Somewhere in a high school

# Thrill Ride

*As the scene opens, BRIAN is sitting on a bench, looking down. KYLE and CHAD ENTER. KYLE looks at CHAD and motions toward BRIAN. KYLE and CHAD walk around the bench and sit on either side of BRIAN.*

#### KYLE

Hey, Brian. You're looking a little down. What's going on?

#### BRIAN

*(Shrugging)* Not much.

#### CHAD

There's your problem. Not much going on—I'd be down too.

#### KYLE

*(Pretending to care)* What, bad weekend or something?

*BRIAN is silent, still looking down.*

#### KYLE

Hey, I thought you had a date last weekend. Who was it ... um ... that freshman. *(He looks over at CHAD and smiles.)*

#### CHAD

Brittle. Her name is Brittle something.

#### BRIAN

*(No enthusiasm)* Brenda.

#### CHAD

*(Smiling)* Yeah, that's it. Brenda.

#### KYLE

So-o-o-o ... you and Brenda didn't hit it off, huh?

#### BRIAN

*(Shrugs)* I don't know ... she's really sweet.

#### CHAD

*(Incredulous)* She's *sweet*? No wonder you're down.

#### KYLE

Chad may have a point there. *(Pause)* Look, there's a party this weekend. Why don't you come? You can bring Brittle too.

#### BRIAN

*Brenda.* I don't think I'll bring a date, thanks.

#### CHAD

No date? What's the point of a party?

#### BRIAN

*(Erupting)* Well what's the point of dating? Why bother? The whole thing is stupid.

#### CHAD

*(Wisely)* Ah, there's your problem. You don't even know what dating is all about.

#### KYLE

Chad's right. There's a very important point to dating.

#### BRIAN

*(Glumly)* Yeah? What?

#### KYLE

Well, dating is like driving. You like to drive, don't you Brian?

#### BRIAN

Sure, who doesn't?

#### KYLE

Well, just like you learned how to drive and you really like it, when you learn what dating is all about, you'll really enjoy it too.

#### CHAD

You just buckle up and enjoy the ride.

#### KYLE

Brian, a girl is like a car. When you've got the right car—well, you just want to get out there and drive. You've been driving the wrong car, that's all.

#### CHAD

And I gotta say, you've been driving some real beaters. Like that girl, Brittle.

#### BRIAN

Brenda. *(Defensively)* She's nice.

#### KYLE

*(Looking from Brian to Chad)* Nice?

#### CHAD

Nice?

#### KYLE

Brenda's the type of girl you marry, not the kind of girl you want to date.

#### BRIAN

What's wrong with that? My mom says you should never date a girl that you wouldn't want to marry.

#### CHAD

There's another problem. You actually listen to what your mom says.

#### KYLE

Look, Brian. Brenda is … well, Brenda is like a station wagon or a nice seven passenger minivan.

#### CHAD

*(Nodding)* Yeah, she's got "family vehicle" written all over her.

#### KYLE

Brian, when you want to settle down, have a family, then look for a nice dependable girl. But right now you need some action.

#### CHAD

You need a sports car, Brian.

#### BRIAN

*(Thinking)* Like a Corvette, or a Ferrari.

#### KYLE

That's it, that's the idea.

#### CHAD

*(Nodding)* Good-looking and fast.

#### KYLE

It doesn't matter if you're driving fast or slow … you're always pushing the speed limits. You follow me?

#### CHAD

Rev it up, baby!

#### KYLE

Get your fill of the thrill.

*KATHY ENTERS. She walks by them and smiles, flirting. KYLE, BRIAN, and CHAD watch as she passes. KATHY EXITS.*

#### KYLE

*(Leaning close to Brian)* Now wouldn't you like to take her for a spin?

#### CHAD

*(Puts hands out like he is holding a steering wheel and driving)* Hug those curves, Brian! Look out for those soft shoulders!

#### BRIAN

*(Skeptical)* Sounds like reckless driving to me.

#### CHAD

You're thinking like your mother again.

#### KYLE

Remember. Dating isn't about finding a girl you want to marry.

#### CHAD

You're not looking for a family car yet.

#### KYLE

You're just looking for something fun—something *really* fun.

#### BRIAN

*(Nodding slowly)* Okay. I'll give it another try.

#### CHAD

Now you're cruisin'.

#### KYLE

Does that mean you're coming to the party?

#### BRIAN

*(Nodding with determination)* Yeah, and I'll bring a date.

#### KYLE

*(Standing and giving BRIAN a friendly slap on the back)* And remember, you're just out for a little joy ride.

#### BRIAN

*(Smiling)* Sounds like more of a thrill ride to me.

#### KYLE

Now you're catching on!

#### CHAD

The ultimate thrill ride! *(Stands to leave.)*

#### KYLE

We'll see you at the party!

*BRIAN stands to leave.*

#### CHAD

And Brian ... no beaters!

*KYLE, BRIAN, and CHAD EXIT, laughing.*

## Thrill Ride

### A Note to the Pastor or Youth Leader:

Life, in many respects, is a lot like dating. Dating allows you to "try out" different people in the hopes of one day finding the person you want to spend the rest of your life with; life allows you to try out different experiences and jobs in hopes of one day settling down in one place or career. In both lies the inherent danger of getting sidetracked from that ultimate goal. The temptation to simply enjoy the pleasures of the present, giving no thought to how it will affect the future is too strong to ignore.

To some degree, focusing on the present isn't a bad philosophy; there is little need for youth—even college students—to be serious about one person or career early in the "trying out" period. But Peter offers some good advice to avoid turning dating—or life—into the thrill ride described in the sketch. Prepare your minds for action, he writes, for all that may befall you in life. Be self-controlled, avoiding temptation even as you experience all that life has to offer. Set your hope fully on the grace given to you, so that you never lose sight of whose you are, and who you are as children of God: His creation, covered by Christ's holy and precious blood.

### Questions for Study and Discussion:

1. How do Kyle and Chad view dating? Do you agree with this philosophy?
2. What is good about their philosophy? What are its dangers?
3. Read 1 Peter 1:13. How does the hope Peter talks about help you when you make the wrong choices?
4. Do you have a dating philosophy? Do you have a life philosophy?
5. Is it possible to enjoy all life has to offer, but still live in accordance to God's commands? How?

# The Edge

**Purpose:** To call attention to some of the dangers inherent in dating and peer pressure

**Theme:** Dating; peer pressure

**Scripture:** 2 Timothy 2:22

**Time:** 5–7 minutes

**Cast:** **Tour Guide**—preferably male, really cares about members of tour

**John**—confident leader

**Jean**—his girlfriend, aggressive, throws caution to the wind, thrill-seeker

**Bob**—enthusiastic, a "me too" kind of guy, rationalizes away caution

**Betty**—his girlfriend, has a real crush on him

**Mike**—smart, appears sincere, but is out to get what he wants, smooth

**Mary**—his girlfriend, has good judgment but can get carried away

**Todd**—demanding

**Tanya**—his girlfriend; she tries to fit in, but deep down is scared

**Costumes:** The four couples wear shorts and T-shirts. The Tour Guide wears something to suggest a "safari" or "park ranger" look

**Props:** Walking stick or a sign with "Tour Guide" printed on it, ring for Mary

**Lighting:** General

**Sound:** No sound effects necessary

**Setting:** The scene takes place at the edge of the Grand Canyon, where a group of four couples is taking a tour. As the scene opens, the Tour Guide has led the group to a scenic overlook of the canyon.

# The Edge

*TOUR GUIDE ENTERS holding walking stick or "Tour Guide" sign. All eight other cast members follow as couples, walking side by side or holding hands. They all look excited.*

### TOUR GUIDE

All right, tour, if you'll step over this way please. *(He motions them to line up so they are all facing the audience, but far from the edge of the canyon.)* Behind me you see the beauty and excitement of the Grand Canyon. This natural wonder is unlike anything you've ever seen or experienced before. I call this spot "Lover's Leap." A word of caution. You will notice there are no railings here. Over that edge is a 200-foot drop to the next level in the canyon. If you go over that edge, you'll be hurting pretty badly. Does everyone understand? *(Others nod. They look a little fearful and back even farther away from the cliff.)* Good. Now, we'll take a short break here while I check in at the park ranger's office. I'll be back in five minutes. *(TOUR GUIDE EXITS.)*

*Group stands there for a moment looking out over the edge. They get up on their tiptoes as they look over the canyon, which is the audience.*

### JOHN

Wow … It's fantastic, huh?

### JEAN

Yeah. It's so exciting!

### BOB

I can't believe we're really here. I've waited my whole life for this!

### BETTY

Me too … *(Turns to look at BOB.)* And I can't think of anyone that I'd rather experience it with.

#### MIKE

*(Taking a couple steps closer to the edge)* Hey, you think it's great back there … you should see it from here! C'mon, Mary, check this out!

#### MARY

*(Stepping up beside him)* Oh, you're right, this is even better!

#### TODD

*(Stepping past MIKE and MARY, even closer to the edge)* Well, if that view is better, then this one will be better yet. *(Looking over edge)* Whoa! Tanya, come here. You've got to experience this!

#### TANYA

*(Stepping up, holding TODD's arm, looking over the edge)* OOOOH, you're right, Todd! *(Turning to the others)* You don't know what you're missing. It's much more exciting here!

*JOHN and JEAN look at each other, nod, hold hands, and step closer to the edge. They are about even with TODD and TANYA. BOB and BETTY hold hands and move up too.*

#### BOB

I was born for this moment!

#### BETTY

Oh, Bob … I'm getting scared! *(She holds him closer.)*

#### BOB

Trust me, Babe. I'd never let anything happen to you.

#### JOHN

*(To JEAN)* Hey, look—all the others are doing it. Let's see how close we can get to the edge! *(He steps forward cautiously to the edge, still holding her hand. He looks over the edge.)* Hey … the tour guide said it was a 200-foot drop. This doesn't look more than 150 feet. I'm beginning to think our tour guide doesn't know as much as we thought.

#### JEAN

Yeah. After all, who is he to tell us what to do?

#### JOHN

We can get closer.

#### JEAN

*(Excited)* Are you sure?

#### JOHN

Trust me.

*JOHN and JEAN are right on the edge. They slide their toes over the edge. Suddenly, they lose their balance and fall. They go screaming to the floor below. They lie there motionless for the rest of the sketch.*

#### BOB

John! Jean! *(Looking over the edge, then back to the group)* They're gone!

#### BETTY

It's awful! *(Pauses, then begins to rationalize)* Well, they did get a little careless. They just didn't know when to stop.

#### BOB

Yeah. We're different, Betty. We're more careful.

#### BETTY

And I can stop anytime I want to.

#### BOB

Me too. I'm in control of myself. *(He loses balance.)* Whoa … WHOA!!

*BOB falls over the edge, still holding BETTY's hand. BETTY follows, screaming. They lie on the floor, motionless, for the rest of the sketch.*

**TODD**

*(Runs to the edge with TANYA)* Bob! Betty! Are you all right?

**TANYA**

*(Worried)* They aren't answering.

**TODD**

They'll be okay. They just need a little time.

**TANYA**

You think so?

**TODD**

I'm sure of it. Hey, this is a total thrill on the edge. Take a step closer. You've got to try this.

**TANYA**

Well, I don't know. The tour guide said …

**TODD**

*(Interrupting)* Tour guide?!? What does he know?

**TANYA**

Well, we're not supposed to go—

**TODD**

Says who? *(Soothingly)* C'mon, Honey … I'm not going to let you get hurt.

**TANYA**

Well … maybe just for a minute. *(She steps to the edge beside TODD.)*

**TODD**

That's my girl. Isn't this exciting?

#### TANYA

*(Getting nervous)* Yeah, but let's go back now.

#### TODD

In a minute. Relax. Enjoy this.

#### TANYA

One more minute, and then we go back, right?

#### TODD

Right. *(He puts his arm around TANYA and loses balance. They both go over the edge screaming, and lie on the floor, motionless, until the sketch is over.)*

*MIKE and MARY run to the edge and look over.*

#### MARY

They're gone!

#### MIKE

It's probably not as bad as it looks. But I could have told you this would happen. Todd wasn't very careful.

#### MARY

What about John? And Bob? Are you saying they weren't careful either?

#### MIKE

Not like I am.

*TOUR GUIDE ENTERS, unnoticed by either MIKE or MARY.*

#### MARY

I say we see how far away we can stay from the edge … not how close we can get to it. *(She lets go of MIKE's hand and backs away from the edge, almost as far as she can go.)*

#### TOUR GUIDE

Good choice, Mary. I knew I could count on you.

#### MARY

*(To TOUR GUIDE)* The others … they all went over the edge!

### Tour Guide

I know. I tried to warn them, but they didn't believe me. This is an exciting view, but it's dangerous too. The whole canyon is full of incredible views and exciting things for you to discover. Don't make this the only thing you see. Don't go back to the edge.

### Mike

There you go again, trying to tell us what we should and shouldn't do. Don't listen to him, Mary. What does he know about having fun? I really like you, Mary. Come out here with me.

### Mary

*(She shakes her head and takes a step backward.)* No. I really like you too, Mike, but don't ask me to go to the edge with you. If you care that much about me, come back here.

### Mike

*(Scooting along the edge, showing off)* You're perfectly safe with me. You just said you care about me ... If you do, prove it by coming to the edge.

### Mary

*(Offended)* Prove it? If you really cared about me, you wouldn't ask me to do *anything*.

### Mike

*(Smooth, convincing)* C'mon, Mary. For me.

*MARY seems tempted for just a moment. She takes a hesitant step forward, then stops to look at the TOUR GUIDE. He gently shakes his head "no." MARY has new confidence and takes a step backward.*

### Mary

I said no. Don't ask me again.

### Mike

*(Proud, intimidating)* Hey, there are a dozen girls who would come out here with me. I guess I was wrong about you. I thought you were special.

### Mary

I *am* special. That's why I'm staying right here. I guess you'll want your ring back. *(She takes ring off finger or necklace.)*

### Mike

*(Angry)* Yeah, I want my ring back. And you'll live to regret the day you gave it back!

*MARY tosses ring to MIKE. He is on the absolute edge, and the action of catching the ring causes him to lose his balance. He goes screaming over the edge, and is silent and motionless on the floor.*

### Mary

Yeah, but I'll live. *(She turns to look at the TOUR GUIDE.)* I'm ready to see the rest of the canyon. Will you lead me?

### Tour Guide

*(Smiles warmly)* I thought you'd never ask.

*TOUR GUIDE and MARY EXIT together.*

# The Edge

## A Note to the Pastor or Youth Leader:

The issues of dating and peer pressure are nothing new to youth or youth leaders. *The Edge* is good as a chapel or Bible study discussion starter to approach these issues once again. After the performance, ask the youth to talk about the characters. Are they realistic? Do the youth know people with similar attitudes? How do they deal with such attitudes? If the youth have actually performed the sketch, ask the actors how it felt to go over the edge. Ask everyone to imagine being in that actual situation (going over the edge of a large canyon). Does it make a difference if we know what awaits us on the bottom? Apply the sketch to the theme of the Bible study (dating, peer pressure, etc.). Where is the edge in our life? Who are the people who lead us to the edge? Who are the people who lead us away from the edge?

The "evil desires of youth" that Paul talks about in 2 Timothy are not limited to youth; they are a result of sin and are inherent in every human from birth to death. They lead us to the edge more times than we can count; and often lead us over the edge.

For both Paul and Timothy, the one hope for forgiveness is Christ. In mercy, Jesus offered Himself as the perfect sacrifice for sins—all sins—and He extends His loving, compassionate hands to pick us up when we fall. Jesus alone is the Savior who cleanses us from guilt and shame. He alone is the Friend and Lord who walks with us, giving us strength to live as His holy people.

Everyone in your group has likely walked to the edge; some have gone over. Together you can ask God's forgiveness in Christ for your sins. Be certain to share the rich, free, and full forgiveness Jesus brings us all.

## Questions for Study and Discussion:

1. What kinds of attitudes do the characters have in approaching the edge?

2. How do these attitudes affect their decisions? The final outcome?

3. Does knowledge of what lies at the bottom of the "canyon" affect their decisions? Would it for you?

4. Where is the edge for you—in dating, peer pressure, life in general?

5. What comfort do you see in 2 Timothy 2:8–10? How does Jesus' forgiveness give you hope in your failures?

# The Palm Reader's Prediction

**Purpose:** To explore some of the things that destroy relationships

**Theme:** Television; relationships

**Scripture:** Colossians 3:1–4; James 1:13–15

**Time:** 5–7 minutes

**Cast:** **Rosa**—a palm reader

**Jason**—a student who is going to the palm reader as a joke

**Lisa**—his girlfriend

**Costumes:** Jason and Lisa wear casual contemporary clothing appropriate to character; Rosa wears stereotypical palm reader clothes, with a lot of jewelry.

**Props:** A small table, candles, two chairs

**Lighting:** General

**Sound:** No sound effects necessary

**Setting:** A palm reading parlor. A small table with candles on it is center stage. Two chairs should be facing each other at opposite ends of the table.

# The Palm Reader's Prediction

*ROSA is sitting at the table waiting for the next customer. JASON and LISA ENTER, holding hands and walking hesitantly toward the table.*

**LISA**

I'm not so sure about this.

**JASON**

Hey, don't back out on me now. You're the one who wanted to know the future.

**LISA**

I just asked you if you would love me forever.

**JASON**

Well ... that's the future. How am I supposed to know?

**LISA**

*(Glancing over at ROSA and whispering loudly)* I didn't expect you'd take me to a palm reader.

**JASON**

*(Shrugging)* You wanted to know the future. I figured we'd see an expert, that's all. *(Smiling)* Come on—this palm reading stuff is all bogus anyway. Let's just have fun with it.

**ROSA**

*(Motioning)* Come in, come in. You have come to have Rosa read your palm, to hear the future, yes?

**JASON**

*(Walking up to the table)* Yeah, I'd like you to read my palm. *(Pointing to LISA)* She just came to watch. Is that okay?

#### Rosa

*(Nods and motions)* Yes, of course. Now sit, sit. *(JASON sits down in the chair. LISA stands behind him, looking over his shoulder.)*

#### Rosa

*(Takes JASON's hand and holds it palm up. She begins to caress his hand gently as she speaks)* Now ... tell Rosa what you would like to know.

#### Jason

Ah ... I thought that was your job.

#### Lisa

*(Bursting in)* He wants to know if we'll always be in love and, you know, get married.

#### Rosa

*(Smiles and nods knowingly, then concentrates on JASON's palm, tracing the lines and creases with the tip of her finger.)* Yes, I see marriage in your future. You will marry a girl you have known for a long time. A high school sweetheart, perhaps.

#### Lisa

*(Squeals with excitement and hugs JASON)* Will we stay together?

#### Rosa

*(Studies palm for a moment.)* Hmmm ... yes, you will walk the path of life together for many years.

#### Lisa

*(Hugging JASON again)* Yes! Will we be happy?

#### Rosa

*(Pauses to look at palm)* There will be good times. *(She frowns as she looks at palm again.)*

**LISA**

*(Sees ROSA's reaction and is concerned)* What is it? What do you see?

**ROSA**

I see a box. One end glows. It will hurt you. It will hurt both of you.

**JASON**

A box that glows? *(Looks at LISA and then back at ROSA)* How will it hurt us? What is it, radioactive or something?

**ROSA**

*(Shakes her head)* No ... the box will influence you.

**JASON**

Influence me? How will that hurt me?

**ROSA**

It will cause you to be dissatisfied with your life. It will cause you to be frustrated.

**JASON**

Huh? What do you mean?

**ROSA**

It will make you desire what you do not have. It will steal precious time from you. It will change you. This will hurt your marriage.

**LISA**

*(Shocked)* Oh, Jason! *(To ROSA)* I don't understand.

**ROSA**

The box will make him desire other women. He will often prefer the company of the box to the company of his wife and his children.

**LISA**

*(Hits JASON)* Oh, Jason ... how could you?

**JASON**

Lisa, this is crazy. If I had some "glowing box" that would take my attention from you, well, I wouldn't even look at it.

*LISA looks over at ROSA as if to see if what he said is the truth.*

**ROSA**

*(Shrugs)* He will look.

**JASON**

What, is someone going to force me to look at it?

**ROSA**

You will look at it willingly. You will sit and look at it for hours.

**LISA**

*(Hits him again)* Jason!

**JASON**

Wait a minute. Hold on for just one minute. So you're saying that there is some "box" in my future. A box with one end that glows. Nobody will force me to look at it, I'll want to. I'll look at it for hours at a time. And somehow, as I look at it, it will influence my thoughts. It may cause me to neglect my wife, or my kids. *(ROSA nods in agreement.)* Well, that's crazy. Why would I ever want some dumb glowing box instead of Lisa?

**ROSA**

The box promises pleasure, but it is not without a price.

**JASON**

And this box, over time, changes my opinions and behavior somehow? *(ROSA nods.)* That sounds like brainwashing to me. You couldn't pay me to look at that box.

#### Rosa

You will pay to watch.

#### Jason

*(Standing and pulling hand from ROSA)* That's it. We're outta here. This palm reading stuff is a bunch of baloney anyway.

*JASON takes LISA by the hand and pulls her toward the exit. LISA makes them stop.*

#### Lisa

Jason, do you think what she said was true ... about the glowing box and all?

#### Jason

Not a chance.

#### Lisa

It gives me a spooky feeling. Let's go to my house. Maybe I'll feel better after we talk about it for awhile.

#### Jason

*(Shaking head)* We don't need to talk about it; we need to forget this whole stupid thing. Let's pick up a video on the way to your place or watch TV.

#### Rosa

*(In a warning tone)* The glowing box already has a grip on your heart.

#### Jason

*(Turning to look at ROSA)* I think you need a grip on reality, lady. That just proves this whole palm reading thing is a hoax ... I don't even have a "box that glows." *(Turns to Lisa, shakes his head and laughs.)* Come on—let's go.

*JASON and LISA EXIT together. After a moment, ROSA EXITS as well.*

# The Palm Reader's Prediction

## A Note to the Pastor or Youth Leader:

This sketch is not meant to condemn television any more than it's meant to condone seeing a palm reader. Rather, its purpose is to introduce some of the things that may destroy relationships, and start a discussion on those things that, as James writes, lead to desire, which leads to sin, which leads, ultimately, to death.

Obviously television doesn't always provide the fun, wholesome entertainment of a generation or two ago. Violence, profanity, and immorality are pumped straight into our living rooms—and that on the evening news. Other shows, while providing a certain amount of educational value, may still pull our focus away from God, our families, and our friends. But television is only one thing among many that works that way in our lives. As we grow in our faith, in our relationships, in our lives, we should be mindful at all times of these things that are seemingly innocent influences on how we act and interact.

Fortunately, we are not left helpless in this task. God works daily in our lives to strengthen and support us in our endeavors and in our relationships. St. Paul provides a remedy to the mindless temptations, by encouraging us to keep our minds on "things above"—the Word of God. And most notably, through Christ's death and resurrection we are forgiven and renewed always, even when we fall away from God, or from our earthly relationships.

## Questions for Study and Discussion:

1. Is television a big part of your life? How about other things, like computers, video games, books, movies, etc.?

2. Are these things all bad? Name both benefits and dangers of each.

3. How might they damage relationships—with friends, family, and God? How might they be used to strengthen relationships?

4. How do you reach a balance between keeping informed in the electronic age, and "setting your mind on things above"?

# The Fabulous Female

| | |
|---|---|
| **Purpose:** | To explore perceptions and misconceptions about women |
| **Theme:** | Women's roles, gifts, and attributes |
| **Scripture:** | Genesis 2:18–24 |
| **Time:** | 5–7 minutes |
| **Cast:** | **Miss Ives**—English teacher; smart, knows her students well |
| | **Jen**—outspoken female student |
| | **Tony**—obnoxious, chauvinistic, thinks he's "God's gift to women" |
| | **Jeff**—ordinary male student, a Christian |
| | **Karen**—a friend of Jen |
| | **Neil**—a friend of Tony |
| | **Students**—other students in the class |
| **Costumes:** | Contemporary clothing appropriate to character |
| **Props:** | Large teacher's desk, individual student desks, books or backpacks for each student |
| **Lighting:** | General |
| **Sound:** | No sound effects necessary |
| **Setting:** | High school English classroom. Teacher's desk is to one side of the stage. Individual desks are set for students so that the audience sees a side view of the class. Desks need to be staggered so the audience has a good view of each student. |
| **Note:** | This script can be used in conjunction with *The Magnificent Male* and *Perfect Combination*. |

# The Fabulous Female

*As the scene opens MISS IVES is seated at her desk and all STUDENTS are seated at their own desks. STUDENTS should each have a stack of books or a backpack at their desks.*

### MISS IVES

*(Stands to address class)* Everyone, please take out the short essay I assigned yesterday.

*JEN takes hers out of her notebook. KAREN looks in her backpack. Other STUDENTS rummage through their papers or backpacks. JEFF lays his on his desk. TONY and NEIL seem confused as to what the assignment was.*

### MISS IVES

The title of your essay was to be "The Fabulous Female ... What Makes Her Unique."

*TONY remembers now. He stands and pulls it out of his pocket. He sits down, unfolds it, and smooths it on his desk. NEIL slouches down in his seat. He obviously didn't write a paper.*

### JEN

Do you want us to pass them to the front?

### MISS IVES

In a minute, Jen. First I'd like to have some of you read yours out loud. *(She looks around the class for a moment.)* Tony ... how about you?

### TONY

*(Enjoys being the center of attention, stands up slowly, shoots a grin at NEIL, and begins to read his paper)* There's a lot I'd like to say about females, but I'll save that for the locker room. *(Looks up for a laugh. NEIL snickers.)* That was a joke, Miss Ives.

### Miss Ives

*(Does not appear amused)* Why don't you save your jokes for the locker room too, Tony.

### Tony

*(Smiles and goes back to reading)* Anyway, what I think you're looking for in this essay is "what makes a female different from a male," besides the obvious differences in anatomy.

*MISS IVES rolls her eyes and nods. KAREN giggles.*

### Tony

*(Reading)* I think the very term *female* says a lot. We all know the root word of *female* is *male*. But what most people don't realize is that the *fe* in female comes from the word in*fe*rior.

*JEN, KAREN, and female STUDENTS protest. NEIL laughs and shakes his head.*

### Tony

Yeah, it's true. The word female literally means "inferior to males."

*Immediate protest from JEN, KAREN, and female STUDENTS.*

### Tony

*(To MISS IVES)* Hey, Miss Ives, do I get to finish or what?

### Miss Ives

*(Looking long and hard at TONY)* Everyone, quiet down. I'd like to hear more of what Tony wrote.

### Tony

*(Grins arrogantly)* Take notes, girls. *(Begins to read again)* This inferiority to males is not my opinion, it's fact. Men are quicker, stronger, have greater endurance, and can pretty much run circles around females in any sport of significance. How many girls do you see in the NFL or Major League Baseball? The

only "fabulous females" on the football field are the cheerleaders! *(Pauses and looks up, grinning)* Am I right, guys? *(NEIL and male STUDENTS laugh, JEN, KAREN, and female STUDENTS roll their eyes, fold arms over their chests, and look disgusted. Reading again)* Females usually go after less physically demanding sports, like volleyball, badminton, and sewing. *(Looks up for a laugh)* Males are smarter too. When's the last time you saw a female mechanic? Most females can't change a tire without the help of a male. Now I wouldn't want you to misunderstand me. I'm not saying females are useless. Who would make the meals, wash the clothes, and clean up around the house? I have a dog at home. Now everyone knows humans are superior to dogs.

#### JEN

*(Interrupting)* Not in your case, Tony!

#### TONY

*(Repeating louder)* Everyone knows humans are superior to dogs, but that doesn't mean I don't want my dog around. And even though females are inferior to males, it's still nice to have them around sometimes ... especially Saturday night, eh, Jen? *(He looks at her.)*

#### JEN

Take your dog out Saturday night, Tony!

KAREN and female STUDENTS cheer. NEIL and the male STUDENTS say "Ooooo."

#### MISS IVES

*(Interrupting)* Thank you, Tony. I think we've heard enough.

#### TONY

But I'm not finished!

#### MISS IVES

*(Glancing at Jen and the other girls)* Oh, I think you are. Sit down.

TONY reluctantly sits down. NEIL leans over and pats him on the back.

#### MISS IVES

I'd like to hear from one of the other males in the room. Do any of you have a different viewpoint? *(She looks around the room and sees no volunteers.)* Jeff, let's hear your essay.

#### JEFF

*(Had been looking down when he was called on. He looks up, obvious dread in his eyes. Reluctantly, he unfolds his paper and stands to read.)* Well, it's kind of short.

#### MISS IVES

That's fine. We don't have much time.

#### JEFF

*(Starts to read)* I think males and females are uniquely different from each other. There are some things I go to my dad for and he's a big help to me. But other things my mom is better at, like listening. If I have a problem or I just need to talk, I always go to my mom. Not that there's anything wrong with my dad. It's just that he always wants to give advice and solve all my problems. Sometimes that's just not what I need. That's why I go to my mom. She listens. She lets me express what I'm feeling, even if it takes hours. I think she represents part of what makes a female different than a male. Females tend to be better listeners, encouragers, and have more patience than males. They can show more love and compassion than males in general.

*JEN, KAREN, and the other female STUDENTS are listening intently. MISS IVES has a slight smile on her face. She nods in agreement as JEFF reads.*

#### TONY

*(Interrupting loudly)* Come on, who wrote this anyway, you or your mother?

*JEN, KAREN, and the other female STUDENTS give TONY a disgusted look.*

#### MISS IVES

Tony, you've had your chance to share. Let Jeff finish, please. *(Turning to JEFF, she nods for him to continue.)* Jeff?

*TONY looks disgusted and slouches down in his chair.*

#### JEFF

*(Glances hesitantly at TONY, then continues.)* Well, my parents make a great team. The way I see it, a man needs a woman as much as a woman needs a man. I guess that makes them equal, but different. Personally, I think the differences in females from males really are fabulous. *(As he finishes, he sits down and folds his paper.)*

#### JEN

*(Sincerely)* That was so sweet!

*KAREN and female STUDENTS nod in agreement.*

#### TONY

*(Bursts out in fake crying)* Oooooooh, that was beautiful, so touching, it makes me sick! *(Makes choking noises.)*

#### MISS IVES

*(Standing)* Thank you, Jeff, for sharing that. Please leave your essays on my desk as you leave. And remember—next week's essay is on "The Magnificent Male."

*JEN, KAREN, JEFF, NEIL, TONY, and STUDENTS stand up and gather their books.*

#### TONY

*(Striking a muscular pose)* "The Magnificent Male." Now that should make for some excellent essays!

*JEN rolls her eyes. JEN, KAREN, NEIL, TONY, and STUDENTS EXIT, followed by MISS IVES.*

# The Fabulous Female

## A Note to the Pastor or Youth Leader:

This sketch should spark some interesting discussion among your group. Many will side with the opinion of their gender in the sketch; others may side with the differing gender's opinion—even some women agreeing with Tony's exaggerated take on things.

As you allow the group to express their opinions, be sure to keep an air of respect for each gender, their different strengths, weaknesses, and roles. Perhaps you may want to talk about how gender roles have changed over the years and why, and why there seem to be some roles or responsibilities that have always remained gender specific. As a conclusion to your discussion, turn to the Genesis account of the creation of the woman. Always mindful of the needs of His creation, God created the woman as a suitable helper to the man so that neither would be alone on their walk through life. Is this still how men and women seem to operate in society today? Is this how your group sees the interaction between men and women?

Throughout the discussion, be mindful of the love and grace God lavishes on all of His creation. After all, although there are many differences between the genders, all of us are sinful beings. Neither gender has the right to claim superiority or supremacy. It is only through the cleansing act of Christ's death on the cross that any of us can be considered worthy in God's sight. His declaration of forgiveness enables us to stand before Him with our fellow humans in a spirit of partnership. We are redeemed, restored. We live and serve together, strengthened by His grace, given in Word and Sacrament.

## Questions for Study and Discussion:

1. Why do you think Tony has the attitude towards females that he does?

2. Do you know people who share Tony's attitude? Do you agree with them? Why?

3. Why do you think Jeff has the attitude toward females that he does?

4. How do men and women balance each other? List some strengths and weaknesses of both.

5. How does God view women? How do you know?

# The Magnificent Male

**Purpose:** Exploring the misconceptions and perceptions about men

**Theme:** Men's roles, gifts, and attributes

**Scripture:** Genesis 1:26–31, 2:7

**Time:** 5–7 minutes

**Cast:** **Miss Ives**—high school English teacher; smart, knows her students well

**Jen**—outspoken female student

**Tony**—obnoxious, arrogant, chauvinistic, thinks he's "God's gift to women"

**Students**—other students in the class; should have male and female

**Costumes:** Students wear contemporary clothing appropriate to character; Miss Ives wears more professional contemporary clothing

**Props:** Large teacher's desk, individual student desks or chairs, books or backpack for each student

**Lighting:** General

**Sound:** No sound effects necessary

**Setting:** A high school English classroom. Teacher's desk is to one side of the stage. Individual desks are set for students so that the audience sees a side view of the class. Desks need to be staggered so the audience has a good view of each student.

**Note:** This script may be used in conjunction with *The Fabulous Female* and *Perfect Combination*.

# The Magnificent Male

*As the scene opens, the MISS IVES is seated at her desk and all the STUDENTS are seated at their own desks. STUDENTS should each have a stack of books or a backpack at their desks.*

### Miss Ives

*(Looking at watch)* All right, class. For the remaining few minutes I'd like you to take out your essays on "The Magnificent Male."

*STUDENTS get busy pulling papers out of notebooks and backpacks. TONY stands up, pulls a folded piece of paper from his back pocket, then sits down and unfolds it noisily.*

### Miss Ives

Do we have any volunteers to read their essay to the class?

### Tony

*(Shoots his hand up fast and high)* Uh, Miss Ives, I'd like to read my essay.

*STUDENTS turn to look at TONY.*

### Miss Ives

I don't think so, Tony.

### Tony

But it's good!

### Miss Ives

I'm sure it is. And if it's anything like your paper on "The Fabulous Female," I'm sure it will generate a lot of class discussion.

### Tony

*(Proudly)* It's better!

#### MISS IVES

Oh, I can just imagine. But I'd like to hear from the girls today. *(TONY slouches down in his chair and folds his arms across his chest.)* Jen, how about you?

#### JEN

*(Picks up her paper and stands up to read)* "The Magnificent Male."

#### TONY

*(Interrupting loudly)* I want you all to know I was Jen's primary resource when she was researching this essay.

#### MISS IVES

Tony! *(Pauses, then nods to JEN to continue.)*

#### JEN

*(Reading)* I don't think the word "magnificent" is the best word to use when describing males. Instead, I would have to say males are more of a wonder to me.

#### TONY

*(Jumping up with excitement)* "Wonder." Excellent choice of a word there, Jen! Males are a wonder, and I'm the most wonderful male you've ever seen!

#### MISS IVES

Sit down, Tony! Let Jen finish.

#### TONY

*(Sits down agreeably. Smiles, puts his feet up and his hands behind his head. Speaks to JEN.)* You go, girl!

#### JEN

*(Looking to find her place on the paper again)* I would have to say males are more of a wonder to me.

*TONY is nodding and raises arms into the air as if he is accepting applause.*

### JEN

I mean, it's a wonder to me that they ever get anywhere or accomplish anything of any lasting value. *(TONY looks stunned.)* Males only have one thing on their mind. They seem to have this major hormone imbalance that totally dominates any logical judgment they might have. This one-track mind of theirs makes them insensitive, insincere, and impatient. I find males to be totally predictable and boring as a result. *(Other female STUDENTS are nodding. TONY is slouched in his chair, sullen.)* Males are a lot like a race car. They can look good and have a lot of power, but all they ever do is go around in circles. The worst thing is that they really don't care. They only care about looking good and sounding good, even if they're going nowhere.

Now if I left it here, I'd be a little unfair to the male sex. There is hope for them. When a lucky male has a good female in his life to focus all that power toward some useful goals, well, then there's almost no limit to his potential. A male can be truly magnificent only with the help of a fabulous female!

*JEN puts paper down, looks toward TONY with a smile of satisfaction, and sits down. Female STUDENTS clap. TONY is still slouched down. Male STUDENTS lean over to talk to him.*

### MISS IVES

*(Smiling)* Thank you, Jen. I must admit many people look at males with that same sense of "wonder."

### TONY

The only "wonder" Jen will ever see is if I ever bother to ask her out again.

### JEN

It would be an even bigger wonder if I ever said yes.

### MISS IVES

Okay, guys. That's enough. We'll pick up on this discussion next week. Please leave your papers on my desk as you leave, and have a good weekend.

*JEN EXITS with female STUDENTS. TONY EXITS with male STUDENTS. MISS IVES shakes her head, smiles, and EXITS.*

# The Magnificent Male

## A Note to the Pastor or Youth Leader:

As with *The Fabulous Female*, this sketch should produce a fair amount of discussion. Remember to mediate in respect to genders and viewpoints.

The viewpoint Jen expresses in her essay is a common stereotype of males. Whether they agree or disagree, have the group try to analyze where it has come from, or how it has developed over the years. Does it fit with the two accounts in Genesis of the creation of man?

The truth is that all of mankind—humankind—is weak and sinful, prone to the same insensitivity and one-mindedness Jen pins on males. We all, male and female, fail to live up to the honor of being created by God, created in the image of God. We all fall prey to the sinful nature inherited after the fall, and treat each other with, at the very least, disrespect and dishonesty. We are thankful, then, that Christ died on the cross and rose again for all of us, men and women. His grace and love are sufficient for all our failings, both because of our gender and in our relations with each other. What's more, washed clean by His blood, we are able again to stand before God as His perfect creation, reflections of His perfect image.

## Questions for Study and Discussion:

1. What is Jen's view of males? What analogy does she use for them? Do you agree?

2. Do you know of others who view males in the same way? How do you think this stereotype developed?

3. If you have used *The Fabulous Female*, how do the two sketches relate? Is one more fair than the other?

4. How does God view men? How do you know?

# Perfect Combination

**Purpose:** To explore how men and women work together

**Theme:** Men and women's roles

**Scripture:** Genesis 1:26–31, 18–24; Ephesians 5:22–33

**Cast:** **Jen**—outspoken female student

**Chris**—her female friend

**Tony**—obnoxious, arrogant, chauvinistic, thinks he's "God's gift to women"

**Jeff**—ordinary student, a Christian

**Students**—five or six students in the class, both male and female

**Costumes:** Contemporary clothing, appropriate to character

**Props:** School desks or chairs, large teacher's desk, books or backpacks for each student

**Lighting:** General

**Sound:** No sound effects necessary

**Setting:** A school classroom. Teacher's desk is to one side of the stage. Individual desks or chairs are set so that audience sees a side view of the class. They should be staggered so the audience has a good view of each student.

**Note:** This script may be used in conjunction with *The Fabulous Female* and *The Magnificent Male*.

# Perfect Combination

*STUDENTS, including TONY, JEN, CHRIS, and JEFF ENTER noisily and gradually find their seats. TONY sits down toward the back of the class by a male STUDENT. JEN and CHRIS sit down near the front.*

### CHRIS

*(To JEN)* I can't believe you turned Tony down for a date again on Saturday.

### JEN

*(Turning so she can look at Tony while she talks to Chris)* I'd never go out with *him* again.

### CHRIS

I still can't believe it.

### JEN

You mean you'd go out with him after what he said about females in his essay?

### CHRIS

*(Smiles and shrugs)* I don't know. He's so cute.

### JEN

Cute? Listen, Chris. There's a lot more a guy has to be than just "cute." I've got a baby nephew—he's cute, real cute. But after a while, you get a little tired of cleaning up his messes and trying to make him happy.

### CHRIS

You're saying that's how it would be with Tony?

### JEN

Uh-huh. Tony doesn't understand girls or really appreciate them for who they are.

#### CHRIS

Maybe you're right, but that's how guys are. You gotta love 'em anyway.

*JEFF ENTERS classroom and sits behind JEN and CHRIS.*

#### JEN

*(Watching JEFF)* I don't think all guys are that way. Take Jeff for example. Remember his essay on "The Fabulous Female"? He's different, or at least he looks at girls a little differently.

#### CHRIS

*(Turning slightly to face JEFF)* Hey Jeff ... what makes you so different?

#### JEN

*(Cringing)* Chris!

#### JEFF

Huh?

#### CHRIS

The way you think about girls. Jen wants to know what makes you so different from other guys.

#### JEFF

*(Thinks for a moment, then shrugs.)* I don't know—maybe the way I was brought up. I grew up understanding that God made man *and* woman. One isn't better than the other, or more important.

#### CHRIS

But what about all that "king of the castle" stuff?

#### JEFF

Well, for the sake of order, God assigned man to be the leader. It only makes sense; someone needs to be the leader. But there's nothing chauvinistic about it. In fact, a good leader sacrifices his life for the ones he leads. God made it pretty clear that a man, as a leader in a husband-and-wife relationship, should sacrifice his life for his wife.

**CHRIS**

*(Incredulous)* You mean "sacrifice" as in die for her?

**JEFF**

*(Laughs)* Well, sort of. I think it means more than that really. "Live for her" is probably more like it.

**CHRIS**

"Live for her"?

**JEFF**

Yeah. Instead of pursuing his own happiness and looking out only for his own best interests, a man should sacrifice that attitude and treat his wife as more important than himself. It really works too. The magnificent male and the fabulous female pair up to make a perfect combination.

**CHRIS**

*(Turns back to look at JEN, confused)* Oh.

*TONY is oblivious to the conversation. He stands and stretches.*

**JEN**

*(Her mind is still on the things JEFF was saying as she turns to talk to CHRIS.)* How romantic!

**TONY**

*(Hears what JEN says and thinks she is speaking about him. He smiles arrogantly and turns the prolonged stretch into a muscular pose. He turns to talk to some of the male STUDENTS.)* Hey, did you hear that? Jen just told Chris she thinks I'm romantic! Well she's a little late. She should have thought of that before she turned me down for that date. Women! Who can figure them out anyway?

*After a beat, JEN, CHRIS, JEFF, TONY, and STUDENTS EXIT.*

# Perfect Combination

## A Note to the Pastor or Youth Leader:

In an age of individualism and political correctness, it's hard sometimes to think of men and women working together as a team. In an age of divorce and pregnancies outside marriage, it's hard sometimes to think of husband and wife working together as a team, or unit. Especially so, it seems, when you've grown up with no concept of how such teamwork develops and benefits the lives of all involved.

It may be hard for members of your group to really understand the perfect combination God intended when creating man and woman. If they have grown up in a single-parent family, or have recently seen their parents or other significant adults in their lives go through painful, bitter divorces, they may see nothing good or beneficial in God's plan. They may even, in some cases, feel guilty that their lives, and their parents' lives, do not fit in with what God intended. Or, in some cases, because they have grown up without such teamwork, feel it's unnecessary in their lives.

But as God said in Genesis, "It is not good for man [and woman!] to be alone." Humans are relational creatures, gaining comfort, strength, support, and growth from interaction with others—especially interaction with members of the opposite sex. Help your group understand the benefits of such relationships. For those living in guilt or anger, bring in the message of the Gospel. All have sinned and fallen short of God's intentions, but His love and grace, demonstrated by Christ's death on the cross, are sufficient for all and beneficial for all in our attempts to work and play on His team, and the teams He creates for us.

## Questions for Study and Discussion:

1. What's the key to Jeff's idea of a perfect combination?

2. Do you agree with Jeff? What's your idea of a "perfect combination"?

3. Read Romans 12:6–8. How does this tie into God's idea of a perfect combination?

4. Does society view marriage in the same way as God? How are they the same? How do they differ?

5. Does a "perfect combination" always mean marriage? What other definitions can it have?

# Emergency Room

| | |
|---|---|
| **Purpose:** | To open a discussion on what happens after death |
| **Theme:** | Life after death; salvation |
| **Text:** | Mark 16:15–16; 1 Timothy 2:1–6 |
| **Time:** | 5–7 minutes |
| **Cast:** | **Mike**—age 17; in hospital with stab wounds |
| | **Mike's Double**—dressed like Mike |
| | **Doctor**—emergency room doctor |
| | **Nurse 1**—emergency room nurse |
| | **Nurse 2**—emergency room nurse |
| | **Nurse 3**—emergency room nurse |
| | **Hooded Figures**—two people dressed in black with hoods pulled low over their faces |
| **Costumes:** | Mike and Mike's Double wear the same contemporary clothes; Doctor and Nurses wear lab coats. Hooded Figures wear black clothes with hoods. |
| **Props:** | A table with a white sheet draping to floor, two paddles with wires attached, other medical-looking instruments if available, a computer monitor if available |
| **Lighting:** | General |
| **Sound:** | No sound effects necessary |
| **Setting:** | The scene is a hospital emergency room, where a doctor and nurses fight to save a 17-year-old stabbing victim. Mike, the victim, has an "out of body" experience and watches as the medical staff works on him. The staff cannot see or hear him as he speaks. They work around Mike's Double to help restrict the audience from getting a good view of the double. |

# Emergency Room

*As the scene opens, MIKE is under the table, hidden from the audience by the sheet. MIKE'S DOUBLE lies on the table, unconscious. NURSES 1, 2, and 3 surround the table, working busily on MIKE'S DOUBLE before the DOCTOR arrives. The monitor is positioned where the nurses can see the screen, but not the audience. The DOCTOR ENTERS, rushing over to the table.*

**DOCTOR**

What have we got?

**NURSE 1**

17-year-old male, multiple puncture wounds.

**DOCTOR**

*(Starts to examine MIKE'S DOUBLE)* Stabbing?

**NURSE 1**

Looks like it. I can't stop the bleeding.

**DOCTOR**

*(Shouting offstage)* We need a type and cross match for 6 units of blood! We need an O.R. right away!

**NURSE 2**

Blood pressure 90 over 50. Respirations are labored.

**NURSE 1**

*(With sense of urgency)* Pulse 120. Heartbeat irregular.

*MIKE slips from under the table. He stands to the side, looking at what's going on.*

**DOCTOR**

*(Determined)* I don't want to lose him.

#### MIKE

You're not going to lose me. I'm right here.

#### DOCTOR

How many times was this kid stabbed?

#### NURSE 3

Eight, by my count. His back, stomach, chest, and throat.

*MIKE reaches for his throat and feels for a wound. The DOCTOR and NURSES are busy working on MIKE'S DOUBLE.*

#### DOCTOR

Anybody know what happened?

#### NURSE 3

A family member said he was hanging out with a rough crowd.

#### MIKE

Rough crowd? Mom must've said that. My friends are a little wild, but that's what I like. I can handle it.

#### DOCTOR

I suppose he thought he could handle it.

#### NURSE 3

Don't they all? Stupid kid.

#### MIKE

Hey—I heard that. Look, I'm fine. Just stitch me up. I want to get out of here.

#### NURSE 3

*(Shaking her head)* Play with fire and you're gonna get burned.

**DOCTOR**

Yep. What goes around, comes around.

**NURSE 3**

Live by the sword and you'll die by the sword.

**MIKE**

Stop with clichés, people. Anyway, who said anything about dying? It's not as bad as you think. I'm *fine.*

**NURSE 1**

His respirations are labored. His lungs are filling up with fluids.

**DOCTOR**

Quick ... suction! *(Shouts offstage)* Get a respirator! Where's the anesthesiologist?

**MIKE**

*(Hands on hips)* You're making it sound a lot worse than it really is.

**DOCTOR**

*(Shaking his head)* Probably a good kid who made some bad choices.

**NURSE 3**

Yeah, like not listening to his mother. I'll bet she warned him. But did he listen? No-o-o. He probably said she was making a big deal out of nothing.

**MIKE**

Come on, lady. You're overreacting.

**DOCTOR**

He probably thought she was overreacting.

**NURSE 3**

I'll bet he'd listen to his mother now.

**NURSE 2**

Blood pressure 90 over 40.

**NURSE 1**

Heartbeat irregular.

**DOCTOR**

*(Shouting offstage)* Get some oxygen over here! *(Continues to examine for a moment.)* He may have been stabbed in the lung. Looks like the knife hit the pericardium. *(Moves to examine the stomach, pushing on it gently.)* His abdomen is filling with blood—get a line in. *(Shouting offstage again)* We need more fluids!

**NURSE 1**

*(Taking pulse of MIKE'S DOUBLE)* Pulse too fast to count, but very faint.

*MIKE checks his pulse.*

**NURSE 2**

I can't get a blood pressure. I can't get a reading.

**NURSE 1**

*(Looking at monitor)* He's in ventricular tack ... make that ventricular fib! Asystole! *(Pronounced "assist-toll-ee")*

**DOCTOR**

*(Taking paddles from nurse)* This is it. Paddles ready—everybody back. Clear! *(Presses paddles against chest.)*

*MIKE'S DOUBLE lurches with the jolt. MIKE also jumps. Surprised, he puts his hand to his heart. HOODED FIGURES ENTER. MIKE watches them suspiciously.*

**NURSE 1**

*(Looking at monitor)* Nothing.

### Nurse 2

Still no reading.

### Doctor

*(With a sense of urgency)* Okay, let's try it again ... Clear! *(Presses paddles to chest again.)*

*MIKE'S DOUBLE lurches. MIKE rubs his chest and winces. HOODED FIGURES walk toward MIKE.*

### Mike

Hey, who are you? You don't look like doctors.

*HOODED FIGURES reach out and grab MIKE by the arms and begin to lead him toward the exit.*

### Mike

*(Resisting a little)* Where are we going? I feel fine. There's nothing wrong with me ... I feel fine!

*HOODED FIGURES EXIT with MIKE.*

### Doctor

We lost him!

### Mike

*(Shouting from offstage)* MAMMA!

*DOCTOR and NURSES stand back slightly from the table. Nurse 2 pulls a sheet over the face of MIKE'S DOUBLE. They look at each other, then one by one, slowly EXIT.*

## Emergency Room

### A Note to the Pastor or Youth Leader:

This sketch is not meant to provide a definitive answer on what happens at the point of death—how we are transported to wherever we will spend eternity. Rather, it is meant to be a discussion starter to bring out possibilities of what happens after death, especially if the person is not a believer.

In Mark 16, Jesus clearly lays out the alternatives. Believe and be baptized and you will be saved; do not believe and you will be condemned. Christ is the only way to salvation, despite what our "do it yourself" society might lead us to believe. Because of these influences of society, and what a youthful spirit—who sees the whole world, his whole life ahead of him—accepts and doesn't accept, Jesus' words are hard to digest. They're even harder to teach when society's opinion prevails, and absolutes are nonexistent.

But Jesus gives us a clear command before laying out the alternatives. Go into the world and preach the Gospel—tell all you meet about the love and grace of God—because there is an absolute ending when you don't believe. The good news is what Paul writes in his letter to Timothy—that God our Savior does indeed want all men to be saved, that He has brought us to Himself, and will guide us as we bring His message to others.

## Questions for Study and Discussion:

1. Describe Mike's attitude at the beginning of the sketch. Did he think anything serious was happening?

2. When did he realize the seriousness of the situation?

3. Can you relate to Mike's feelings? Why?

4. What comfort can you take from the message in 1 Timothy 2:1–6, especially verse 4?

5. Are you willing to share that comfort with others? What is the importance of doing so?

# The Truth about Hell

**Purpose:** To open a discussion on the reality and misconceptions of hell

**Theme:** Hell

**Scripture:** 2 Thessalonians 1:5–12

**Time:** 5–7 minutes

**Cast:** **Eddie**—high school student; proud, cynical, and self-confident

**Mom**—his mom

**Carla**—his younger sister; she can never stand up to him

**Ron**—his friend; the follower to Eddie's leader

**Costume:** Contemporary clothing, appropriate to character

**Props:** Two chairs, TV remote control

**Lighting:** General

**Sound:** No sound effects necessary

**Setting:** The family room of Eddie's home. The two chairs are set up next to each other, facing the audience. An actual TV or a box to represent one can be set between the audience and the chairs.

**Note:** This sketch is to be used in conjunction with *The Truth about Heaven* and *Getting There*.

# The Truth about Hell

*As the scene opens, EDDIE is sitting in one chair, CARLA in the other. CARLA is holding a TV remote and is trying to watch her program. MOM ENTERS.*

#### MOM

Eddie, Ron is at the door.

#### EDDIE

*(Looking at the TV)* Great. Have him come in here.

MOM EXITS. A moment later RON ENTERS.

#### RON

*(Taking off coat)* Hi, Eddie.

#### EDDIE

Hi, bum. Grab a chair. *(He motions toward chair CARLA is in. CARLA tries to ignore RON while he stands there awkwardly. To CARLA)* Move it.

#### CARLA

Hey, I was here. I'm watching TV.

#### EDDIE

*(Smoothly snatches remote from her hand and turns off the TV)* Not any more.

#### CARLA

*(Whines)* Eddie!

#### EDDIE

Excuse me, we have a guest here. Where are your manners?

#### CARLA

*(Stands abruptly)* I'm telling Mom.

#### EDDIE

Hey, while you're talking to her, ask her to bring us a couple of Cokes. *(CARLA is standing there fuming as RON sits in her chair. He puts his jacket over the arm of the chair. EDDIE immediately scoops up Ron's jacket and tosses it to CARLA.)* And hang up our guest's jacket too. *(CARLA catches jacket and angrily EXITS. Turning to RON)* So, did your mom make you go to church again yesterday?

#### RON

Yeah. I promised her I'd go for four weeks.

#### EDDIE

Well?

#### RON

Well what?

#### EDDIE

*(Thinking this whole thing is funny)* What did the preacher talk about?

#### RON

Most of the time he talked about hell.

#### EDDIE

*Hell?*

#### RON

Yeah. It kind of made me think. Do you ever think about hell?

#### EDDIE

*(Making a sarcastic play off the word)* Hell, no! *(He smiles. He is pleased with his little pun.)*

#### RON

*(Catches Eddie's little joke and smiles.)* Well, do you believe there is such a place?

#### EDDIE

I sure hope so.

#### RON

*(Puzzled)* You hope so?

#### EDDIE

Yeah. You can't picture me sitting on a cloud with a little harp, can you?

#### RON

*(Laughing)* No.

#### EDDIE

*Hell,* no! Hey, I'm looking forward to hell. *(Leans forward, really getting into it.)* Think about it. You won't need a coat anymore. It will be like summer all year around. I'll probably have a motorcycle—no, make that a convertible. I'll do whatever I want and I'll never get carded. It will be one big party. All our friends will be there, and all the girls will wear bikinis. I'm telling you, I wouldn't miss it. It'll be great!

#### RON

Gee, it sounds like you're planning the ultimate vacation.

#### EDDIE

I am. It will be like paradise. I mean, hey, it beats sitting on a cloud. Am I right?

#### RON

*(Laughs, shakes head)* You're crazy, Eddie. *(EDDIE smiles proudly and leans back in his chair with his hands behind his head.)* But the preacher yesterday said hell isn't like that. He told us some of the examples the Bible uses to try to describe it, and none of them sounded very good to me.

#### EDDIE

Yeah? Like what?

#### RON

A "lake of fire."

#### EDDIE

*(Unaffected by the description, amusing himself with his wit)* Hey, babe ... surf's up! What else?

#### RON

You know that feeling you get when you're asleep and you think you're falling? Well, hell is described as a bottomless pit. It's like you'll always be falling.

#### EDDIE

The ultimate bungee jump. Sounds like fun. What else?

#### RON

The skin will melt right off people and they'll grind their teeth in pain, but they won't die. If any girl is wearing a bikini, she won't be worth looking at.

#### EDDIE

Anything else?

#### RON

Well, he said people would be weeping.

#### EDDIE

They do that at reunions, you know. Happy to see each other and all that. What else?

#### RON

I don't remember much else. It just made me think, that's all.

#### EDDIE

Well, *I* think you should *stop* thinking. Let's get the *hell* out of here and have some fun. *(MOM ENTERS. Both EDDIE and RON are just standing up to go.)* We're going out for awhile, Mom.

### Mom

Okay, Honey. Don't be late.

*EDDIE starts to leave, has a thought, then turns back to MOM.*

### Eddie

Hey, Mom, do you suppose Dad's going to heaven when he dies, or going to hell?

### Mom

Oh, I'm sure he'll be in hell. He didn't believe in God; that's one of the reasons I divorced him.

### Eddie

*(To RON as they start to leave)* See? I'll even get to see my dad for more than just the holidays!

### Ron

*(Shakes his head and laughs)* You're crazy, Eddie!

*EDDIE and RON EXIT.*

# The Truth about Hell

## A Note to the Pastor or Youth Leader:

A discussion of hell may seem strange to youth today. Many people simply reject the idea of hell; others "change" hell into any place or time of suffering and pain during this earthy life. Yet the Scriptures are clear: the place where unbelievers will be punished forever is real. All who reject God and His offer of free and full forgiveness in Christ will be condemned—that is, banished from God's eternal presence and confined to darkness and torment and separation. All who reject God will "go to hell."

Why mention hell? Why think about hell? God is a holy God. The one true God is a righteous God, who created human beings and still commands us to obey His Word and follow His ways. By nature all people rebel against God. We reject His claim on our lives and choose our own paths—sin, alienation, and hostility. The holy, righteous God must deal with sin; God must carry out His threat to punish sinners.

The Gospel proclaims God has dealt with sin and sinners in the saving work of His Son Jesus. Jesus takes on Himself the punishment we deserve, and He dies our death to redeem us from the Law. In Him we are forgiven. Through faith in Jesus we stand holy, righteous before God, and our heavenly Father welcomes us to eternal glory—in heaven!

Hell is real. We can and should convey this truth in our witness to our faith, pointing to the holy God who threatens punishment. But above all we focus on the Gospel—salvation in Christ—as the promise of salvation and life with God in heaven.

## Questions for Study and Discussion:

1. Describe the difference between Eddie and Ron as they think about hell. Which view do you see most often among your friends and acquaintances?

2. What do you think about hell?

3. What comfort does Christ give you about punishment?

# The Truth about Heaven

**Purpose:** To open a discussion on the realities and misconceptions about heaven

**Theme:** Heaven

**Scripture:** Romans 8:18

**Time:** 5–7 minutes

**Cast:** **Eddie**—high school student; proud, cynical, and self-confident

**Mom**—his mom

**Ron**—his friend; the follower to Eddie's leader

**Costumes:** Contemporary clothing, appropriate to character

**Props:** Two chairs, TV remote control

**Lighting:** General

**Sound:** No sound effects necessary

**Setting:** The family room of Eddie's home. The two chairs are next to each other, facing the audience. An actual TV or a box to represent one can be set between the audience and the chairs.

**Note:** This sketch is to be used in conjunction with *The Truth about Hell* and *Getting There*.

# The Truth about Heaven

*EDDIE is slouched in a chair, holding the remote control, watching TV.*

### Mom

*(Calling from offstage)* Eddie, Ron's here to see you.

### Eddie

*(Turning off the TV with the remote)* Okay, Ma ... send him in here.

*RON ENTERS.*

### Ron

*(Walks in smiling, peels off coat, tosses it on the empty chair, and flops down.)* Hey, Eddie. What were you watching?

### Eddie

Nothing decent. Mom's still home. *(He smiles.)* So, hey, tell me, what did the pastor say yesterday, or didn't you go?

### Ron

Yeah, I went. You should have gone with me. He talked about heaven.

### Eddie

*(Disgusted)* Heaven! I'm glad I didn't let you talk me into it. I already missed the one I wanted to hear.

### Ron

Which one was that?

### Eddie

The one about hell. That would be a little more my speed.

**RON**

*(Shaking head)* You're crazy, Eddie.

**EDDIE**

Okay, so what did he say about heaven?

**RON**

Well, it's going to be incredible.

**EDDIE**

What—harps, choirs, wings on shoulders? Sounds real incredible. *(Rolls his eyes.)* Right!

**RON**

No, it's nothing like that. It'll be better than anything you could ever experience here on earth.

**EDDIE**

Hey, I can imagine some experiences right here on earth that will beat heaven any day. *(Leans forward. He enjoys being the cynic and controlling the conversation. He especially enjoys his new angle of reasoning.)* Let me ask you something. Did the pastor say there would be sex in heaven?

**RON**

What?

**EDDIE**

You heard me. Will there be sex in heaven?

**RON**

*(Confused)* Ah, I don't think so Eddie.

#### EDDIE

*(Sits back, puts hands behind head, and smiles smugly)* I rest my case, unless you're saying heaven will be better than sex.

#### RON

Did I say that?

#### EDDIE

Sure you did. You said heaven is better than anything I could imagine on earth. If there is no sex in heaven, that means heaven would have to be better than sex, right?

#### RON

Well, yeah, I guess so. I never thought of it that way before.

#### EDDIE

I rest my case. The whole thing sounds impossible. I can't imagine there could be anything better than what sex would be like. So why would I want to go to heaven? I'd rather find a little "heaven on earth."

*RON sits back. He is thinking and appears to be stumped. He starts to get an idea and sits forward. Up to this point, EDDIE has been able to control things by his cocky attitude and opinions. Now RON begins to come back with reasoning that can't be passed off so lightly. RON starts to gain control of the conversation here, and EDDIE is uncomfortable with that.*

#### RON

Eddie, remember what you thought about girls when you were about 10 years old?

#### EDDIE

Yuck.

#### RON

Okay ... and what did you think about sex?

#### EDDIE

I didn't think about it then. *(Trying to lighten things up)* But I sure made up for lost time, eh?

#### RON

C'mon Eddie, I'm serious. Now think. When your mom and dad first told you about the birds and the bees, what did you think of the idea that your parents had sex?

#### EDDIE

Gross!

#### RON

Exactly. And what do you think about it now?

#### EDDIE

My parents having sex? Gross!

#### RON

No—what do you think about sex now?

#### EDDIE

Well ... I don't think it's gross anymore. I imagine it's about the best thing earth has to offer.

#### RON

*(Getting more excited as his argument takes shape)* Right! Now listen. God *made* sex.

#### EDDIE

Huh?

#### RON

Think about it. God was the inventor of it.

#### EDDIE

*(Suspicious)* Yeah.

#### RON

So God says we can't imagine what heaven is like, it's so far beyond anything that can be experienced on earth. It's like when you were a kid, you thought sex sounded gross, but now the idea of it sounds real good.

#### EDDIE

Okay, so I was wrong.

#### RON

Real wrong. And now you think heaven is boring. You may be wrong again. I mean, the guy who invented sex is saying "You ain't seen nothing yet."

#### EDDIE

*(RON has made sense. EDDIE is clearly thinking, and for a moment he is serious.)* I can't imagine that.

#### RON

Exactly. You have to trust the One who invented sex that there is something even better ... and it's in heaven.

*Both RON and EDDIE sit quietly for a moment. EDDIE is struggling with the truth. EDDIE pushes back the truth and runs from it.*

#### EDDIE

You know what I think?

#### RON

What.

#### EDDIE

You're not as much fun when you think so much. *(Getting up)* C'mon, let's go raid the refrigerator.

*EDDIE EXITS. RON is still sitting in the chair. He is disappointed that EDDIE won't listen.*

#### EDDIE

*(Calling from offstage)* Hey, Ron—hurry, you'll love this.

#### RON

What is it?

#### EDDIE

My mom made angel food cake!

#### RON

*(Stands up, shakes his head)* Eddie, you're crazy!

*RON EXITS.*

# The Truth about Heaven

## A Note to the Pastor or Youth Leader:

"I consider that our present sufferings are not worth comparing with the glory that will be revealed in us," Paul writes in Romans 8:18. He knows a good thing when God speaks it. From the beginning of time God has prepared a place of joy and blessing for those who are called according to His purpose in Christ. Heaven is our true home. To be in the presence of the Savior is the goal of our journey through life on earth. God's people confidently endure the hardships and pain of this world because Christ has won for us on the cross the victory over sin, death, and the devil.

But "all roads" do not lead to heaven. Because of sin, human beings cannot earn their way into heaven by their works; they cannot find their way to heaven with their own wisdom or knowledge. By nature we are dead in trespasses and sin, and we have no claim to live with God forever in glory.

The only hope for heaven is Jesus Christ. On the night before His death, Jesus shared the one solid road to heaven: "I am the way and the truth and the life. No one comes to the Father except through Me" (John 14:6). Thanks be to God for His Son, who came from heaven to rescue us from sin, death, and the power of the devil.

## Questions for Study and Discussion:

1. Describe how Ron was impacted by the sermon on heaven.

2. Do you think Eddie really understands what heaven is all about? Why?

3. What misconceptions about heaven have you heard?

4. What do you most look forward to about heaven?

# Getting There

**Purpose:** To emphasize the importance of faith in Christ

**Theme:** Salvation through Christ alone

**Scripture:** Colossians 1:13

**Time:** 5–7 minutes

**Cast:** **Ron**—high school student; has been wrestling with the issues of heaven and hell

**Mom**—his mom; she has been taking him to church

**Eddie**—Ron's friend; rejects what Ron has been trying to tell him

**Pastor**—the pastor or youth pastor at the church Ron has been attending

**Costumes:** Ron wears pajamas or a T-shirt and shorts; the rest should wear contemporary clothes, appropriate to character

**Props:** A cot or table, blankets, pillow, small nightstand, lamp, TV and VCR

**Lighting:** Lights will need to be adjusted throughout the sketch

**Sound:** Amplification of TV and VCR

**Setting:** Ron's bedroom. The cot (or table made up like a bed) is center stage, parallel to edge of stage. The TV and VCR are behind the bed, toward the foot, facing the audience. For this sketch to be effective, part of it needs to be done ahead of time and videotaped with a home video recorder. At the appropriate time, the TV in Ron's room will be used to play the tape (Ron's dream) while Ron sleeps.

**Note:** This sketch is to be used in conjunction with *The Truth about Hell* and *The Truth about Heaven*.

# Getting There

*RON ENTERS, dressed for bed.*

### Ron

*(Starting offstage, calling loudly)* Goodnight, Mom. I'm going to bed.

### Mom

*(From offstage)* All right, Dear. Sleep well.

### Ron

*(Walking toward bed)* I will.

### Mom

And Ronnie?

### Ron

Yeah, Mom?

*MOM ENTERS, pausing at the entrance to room.*

### Mom

Ronnie, just think about what the pastor said last night.

### Ron

*(In a "don't push me" tone)* Mom—

### Mom

I know, I know, I won't push. Just tell me you'll think about what he said, even for a little while.

### Ron

*(Smiles.)* Okay, Mom. *(Climbs into bed.)* How can I *not* think about it? He was pretty direct with all that heaven and hell stuff.

#### Mom

Thanks, Honey. Sleep well.

#### Ron

*(Getting comfortable in bed)* I will. Would you turn out the light when you go out?

#### Mom

Sure, Ronnie. Goodnight. *(Starts to leave, turns back, and whispers loudly enough for audience to hear.)* Think about it.

*MOM EXITS. Lights turn off except the lamp by the bed.*

#### Ron

*(Propped up on one elbow, talking to himself)* Yeah, I'll think about it. I can't get that pastor's voice out of my head. *(He lies down on his side, facing the audience, and closes his eyes. He pulls a blanket up to his chin and is still.)*

*VIDEO begins to play on the TV. This can be turned on by someone offstage or by RON from a remote. VIDEO FADES in to a close view of the PASTOR preaching from the pulpit.*

#### Pastor

Hell isn't going to be a picnic or a party. It's going to be like a horrible nightmare, but you'll never wake up.

Imagine life as a long hallway with doors on both sides. Many of the doors claim to be the way to heaven. If you choose them—like choosing ones marked "fame and fortune" or "doing it my way"—they may bring you some amount of satisfaction. But as a way to heaven? No. Ultimately they will lead to hell. There's only one way to heaven, and that's through Jesus.

*VIDEO FADES OUT and FADES IN to a new scene as RON tosses on his bed a little, and pulls the covers over his head. Now his back is to the audience so he can peek at the TV and jump out of bed at the right time. As the next scene begins, RON will use the blanket over his head to cover his own actions as the video plays. RON has a plastic bag with a very wet sponge in the bed with him. RON uses the sponge to give himself a "sweaty nightmare" look. He should sponge himself around the neck, down the middle of the chest to the stomach, under the arms of the T-shirt or pajama top, on his face and the hair around the ears. This has to be done carefully so the audience is not distracted.*

*The next video scene is set in a long hallway of a hotel, apartment building, or condo. Any of these will do, as long as there is an elevator.*

*RON is going down the hall, dressed as he is in bed. He moves down the hall, slowly at first, looking at each door he passes. He hesitates at one door, then appears to change his mind and hurries on to the next one. He almost knocks on one door, but stops suddenly and runs to the next one. He appears to panic as he picks up speed, running from door to door. RON runs to the elevator. The video camera is close now. RON is panting, there is fear in his eyes.*

*RON moves for the elevator button. Shoot close-up of his hand hesitating at the "up" and "down" buttons. He deliberately pushes the "up" button two or three times. The video returns to a full shot.*

*If you can do a voice-over or dubbing with your equipment you may want to dub in the PASTOR's voice while RON is going from door to door. The voice might say, "Life is like a long hallway with a lot of doors. You can pick any number of doors ... but they all go to the same place ... they all lead to hell. Without Jesus ... you're going to hell ...You're going to hell ... You're going to hell ... You're going to hell ..." The dubbing should end by the time RON gets to the elevator.*

## Ron

*(Nervous, impatient)* I want Jesus ... I want Jesus. *(Looking anxiously at elevator doors)* C'mon ... C'mon *(Pushing the "up" button frantically)* I need Jesus ... I need Jesus.

*The elevator doors begin to open. RON looks relieved and moves toward them. RON stops abruptly as he sees his friend EDDIE inside. EDDIE needs to hold the "door open" button while this is being taped.*

## Ron

*(Incredulously)* Eddie?!?

## Eddie

*(Giving an evil smile)* Hi-ya, bum. Going down?

#### RON

*(Backing away)* No ... NO! I want to go up. I want to go to heaven!

#### EDDIE

*(Smoothly)* Too late for that, Ron. You're going to HELL!!

#### RON

*(Covering ears)* No! NO! *(Fearfully)* You're crazy, Eddie. I want Jesus—I need Jesus!

*VIDEO FADES to black.*

#### RON

*(Immediately RON throws back covers from the bed and leaps to his feet, screaming)* I NEED JESUS! I NEED JESUS! *(Stands there panting.)*

*MOM ENTERS. She rushes in with a robe on. She flips on the lights. She is worried.*

#### MOM

Ronnie, Honey—what's wrong?

#### RON

*(Sits on the edge of the bed)* Bad dream. Very bad. Intensely bad dream.

#### MOM

*(Hesitantly)* Do you know what you were shouting?

#### RON

*(Nods)* Yeah—"I need Jesus." *(Pause)* I really do, don't I, Mom?

#### MOM

*(Giving him a hug)* Yes, Honey, you really do. We all do. Would you like to go downstairs for a snack and talk about it?

### Ron

*(Nods thoughtfully)* Yeah, I'd like that. *(He stands)* And Mom?

### Mom

Yes, Honey?

### Ron

Let's get your Bible too.

*MOM smiles, puts her arm around RON. MOM and RON EXIT.*

## Getting There

### A Note to the Pastor or Youth Leader:

Like many young adults, Ron is searching for the truth—the truth about eternity. He is restless to know what God has reavealed in His Word about heaven and hell, yet is torn by the "ways of the world," represented by Eddie. Perhaps Ron's struggle illustrates the struggles we all often face: to believe God, to take seriously His threats, and to trust His promise in the midst of temptation and pressure.

God threatens to punish sinners, it is true, but His heart—His desire and purpose—is to save all people. The many doors we encounter in life—pleasure, wealth, success, status—conspire to lead us away from the one true door to heaven. Our sinful nature draws us to acts opposed to God's holy will and ways. On our own we stand condemned, deserving hell.

Yet Christ in His love and mercy came from heaven to "seek and to save" the lost and condemned. The Savior of the world rescues us from the "dominion of darkness," as Paul writes in Colossians, and brings us into the kingdom of His love. Christ Jesus is the only "door" we have—indeed, the only door we need—to get "there," eternal life in heaven.

## Questions for Study and Discussion:

1. Describe Ron's anxiety. In what ways have you experienced anxiety over heaven and hell?

2. To whom can you most relate: Ron or his mother? Why?

3. What doors—open or closed—work to draw you away from God?

4. Share how Christ removes our fear of death and hell.

5. Who in your life "needs Jesus" and His saving love and forgiveness?

# Lisa's Letter

**Purpose:** To explore consequences of premarital sex not often discussed

**Theme:** Premarital sex; relationships; dating

**Scripture:** 1 Corinthians 6:12–20

**Time:** 5–7 minutes

**Cast:** **Lisa**—a former high school student

**Costumes:** Casual contemporary clothing

**Props:** A stool, a piece of paper

**Lighting:** A spotlight, if available

**Sound:** Microphone, if needed

**Setting:** Bare stage, except for the stool and microphone stand

# Lisa's Letter

*As the scene opens, a disclaimer statement may be read: "The character in this sketch is purely fictitious. Any resemblance to a particular individual is purely coincidental." LISA is sitting on the stool with a single light to keep the attention focused on her.*

### LISA

Hi, my name is Lisa. A friend from school brought me to this youth group a number of years ago, and I really enjoyed it. I became a Christian here, after hearing how God loved me and how He gave His Son to die for my sins. And after a while, I really began to grow—you know, trusting God more and making Him a real part of my daily life.

But that's not what I want to talk about tonight. See, God isn't the only one I met here; I also met John. *(Pauses.)* I've collected my thoughts on paper. I hope you don't mind if I read them; I won't be quite as nervous that way.

*She continues as though reading a letter. She "reads" with expression, varying volume. She looks up occasionally and pauses when appropriate.*

John was cute, and nice, and a Christian too. In a very short time after we started going out, I knew there was nobody else on earth with whom I'd rather spend the rest of my life. He felt the same way; I can't tell you how many times he talked about marrying me. If we weren't on the phone together, we were with each other. We spent a lot of time alone together; too much time. Usually, he'd come over to my house, and my parents were rarely home.

It wasn't long before we started having problems physically. Technically, we never had intercourse, but we came as close to it as we could. And although I probably wouldn't have admitted it to myself at the time, what we were doing was still sex. Now, I didn't get a sexually transmitted disease, or get pregnant, or have an abortion. But the devastation in my life and in John's was just as real as if one of those did happen.

Both of us being Christians, well, we knew God had designed sex to be reserved for marriage. As we started getting more and more involved physically, we struggled with guilt. We'd tell each other and ourselves that we'd never go that far again. We tried making little resolutions, you know, like "From now on we'll never go past such and such point physically." Well, we both broke those "resolutions" as many times as we made them.

Sex added a level of tension to our relationship that never should have existed. When John would pick me up for a date, his hormones were already racing. He'd be anticipating our date together and the pleasure he expected to enjoy. I was just happy to be with him; it was more of an emotional thing with me. But if I held the line and didn't give in to his sexual advances, he'd get real frustrated and our date would end up in a huge argument. If I did give in, we'd both be frustrated that we'd failed once again, and we'd get into an argument anyway.

It's ironic how sex works. When a couple is married, sex is part of the glue that keeps them close, holds them together. But when you're dating ... well, sex was tearing us apart. It was ruining our relationship.

For a while I'd push the guilt away. I'd think, "Hey, we failed tonight, but I'll do better tomorrow." Or, "Technically, we didn't have intercourse, and we're planning to marry, so it's really not so bad." But you can only play those mind games so long. Our arguments grew worse and I don't know how many times we broke up.

Every time we'd get back together, we'd soon be back to our old ways. John was consumed by sex, and this preoccupation started putting more distance between us.

I knew sex was designed to be the most fantastic wedding present from God. At the very least, I had cheated and opened the present early. Even if John and I were to be married, we had jumped the gun. The present that would have brought me total ecstasy if I were married, was weighing me down with guilt.

But what if John and I weren't to be married? I had never considered that. What if God had someone else in mind for me? The thought panicked me. If that were the case, I had done more than simply open the present early. If John wasn't to be my husband, then God had prepared me as a present for a different guy, probably someone I hadn't even met yet.

That would mean I had let John unwrap the present God had intended as a gift for my future husband. Someday, I would have to offer this present to the man who would commit his entire life to me, and I would have to give it to him slightly used.

Eventually, John and I broke up for good. I'm convinced it was the sex and all the guilt and pain that went with it that finally destroyed us. When the word was out that John and I were through, other guys showed interest. But I could never be sure if it was because they really liked me, or if they knew I'd been sexually active. They didn't get anything from me though, and none of them stayed around very long.

I didn't want to hurt like I did with John ever again, so I developed a personal code of conduct for dating. I did it too late for John and me, but I've used it ever since:

1. Dates must be well planned. If there's just a lot of time together and no real plans, things could easily get physical.

2. Avoid being alone together. No more being at a guy's house or him at my house when nobody else is home. We can be alone in a crowd, like a restaurant, and we won't be tempted. The same goes for the car. I'll never sit in a parked car and talk. It only leads to trouble.

3. Don't go to see or rent any movies that are likely to show skin and arouse us sexually.

4. Don't unbutton, unsnap, unzip, or remove any clothing from each other.

5. Don't let any guy touch any place from my shoulders to my knees. I need to keep my hands off my date too. I'm really careful even when I'm kissing that we don't get too carried away.

There are other things I'm very careful of now, but those were some of the main ones.

If a guy asked me out more than once, I shared my dating standards with him. Some never called back. Others took me as kind of a challenge. They lost.

It's been years since John, but I still have a lot of scars. I don't think he ever fully recovered either. We were in love, but we destroyed our relationship by expressing our love in such a physical way.

I'm not proud of what I did with John. I wish I had never compromised sexually; I lost some of the best years of my life. I wish I could go back and relive those years, differently this time, but I can't.

Recently, I met a good Christian guy I hope to marry someday. We've been tempted, but we're doing well, and I'm pretty proud of that.

Well, I hope something I've said will help save someone here from all the pain I went through. Thanks for listening.

*LISA stands and puts her paper down. She looks at the audience for a moment and then EXITS.*

## Lisa's Letter

## A Note to the Pastor or Youth Leader:

Start talking about sex, and more than likely you'll have your group interested. Start talking about some of the typical problems associated with sex (pregnancy, diseases), and more than likely you'll have people tune out. "Yeah, yeah, yeah," they say. "We know all about those types of problems—everyone tells us about those problems. Who cares anymore?" The types of problems Lisa talks about, however, aren't discussed nearly as often. And more than likely, they're the ones people in your group will be thinking about the most. Pregnancy is a real issue, yes—but very remote. Guilt, frustration, anger, remorse—these issues are much more real, much more apparent in your group's daily grapple with the temptations of sex.

In one sense, reading the passage in 1 Corinthians only adds to the guilt. Our bodies are temples of God—whatever dishonorable thing we do with them dishonors God, as if we didn't displease Him enough already in our other daily activities. But on a second reading, the verses provide additional fuel to fight temptation. We are created by God, our bodies—not just our souls, but our bodies also—belong to Him, and are dwelling places for His Spirit. Such dignity this brings us—such pride we can take in what God has created us to be! We do not need sex to give us that belonging, that false sense of pride that people often look for. The real thing is ours by virtue of our redemption: "You were bought with a price." (1 Corinthians 6:20).

The guilt, shame, remorse, frustration, and other feelings that arise from misusing God's gift (both sex and our bodies) are real feelings that need to be addressed. As Lisa states, these feelings started to affect her relationship; they affect many other things as well. God's saving grace through Jesus' death and resurrection washes us clean from these feelings and helps us consider how we can live differently, more in tune with God's will.

## Questions for Study and Discussion:

1. What did Lisa cite as the reasons that she and John began to deepen their relationship physically?

2. How did Lisa and John's sexual experimentation affect their relationship? How did it affect Lisa?

3. What caused their breakup?

4. Do you think their problems and temptations are typical of problems today? Why?

5. How do you feel about Lisa's code for dating?

6. How do you feel about being a temple of the Holy Spirit? About honoring God with your body?